# Life Around the World
# Birthdays in Many Cultures

**Martha EH Rustad**

raintree
a Capstone company — publishers for children

Raintree is an imprint of Capstone Global Library Limited, a company incorporated in England and Wales having its registered office at 264 Banbury Road, Oxford, OX2 7DY – Registered company number: 6695582

**www.raintree.co.uk**
myorders@raintree.co.uk

Edited by Sarah L Schuette
Designed by Kim Brown and Alison Thiele
Picture research by Wanda Winch
Originated by Capstone Global Library Ltd
Printed and bound in China

ISBN 978 1 4747 3537 7
20  19  18  17  16
10 9 8 7 6 5 4 3 2 1

**British Library Cataloguing in Publication Data**
A full catalogue record for this book is available from the British Library.

**Acknowledgements**
Alamy: Cultura Creative, 11, david hancock, 5, Edwin Remsberg, 7; Capstone Studio: Karon Dubke, cover, 1; Getty Images: Niedring/Drentwett, 9; iStockphoto: Denisfilm, 13; Newscom: VARLEY/SIPA, 15; Shutterstock: Rabus Carmen Olga, 19, XiXinXing, 21; The Image Works, 17

Every effort has been made to contact copyright holders of material reproduced in this book. Any omissions will be rectified in subsequent printings if notice is given to the publisher.

All the Internet addresses (URLs) given in this book were valid at the time of going to press. However, due to the dynamic nature of the Internet, some addresses may have changed, or sites may have changed or ceased to exist since publication. While the author and publisher regret any inconvenience this may cause readers, no responsibility for any such changes can be accepted by either the author or the publisher.

# Contents

# Birthday parties

People celebrate
their birthdays
in many cultures.

North
America

Europe

Asia

Africa

South
America

Australia

🎂 Australia

People play games
on their birthdays.
A girl in Mexico
breaks open a piñata.

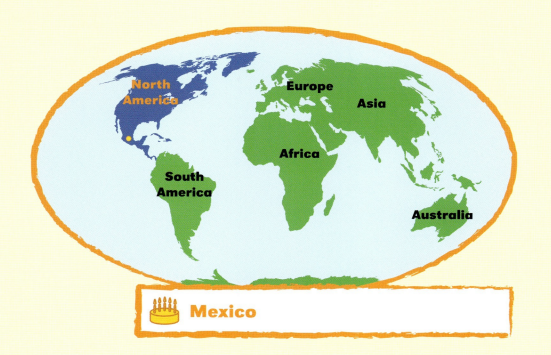

🎂 Mexico

A girl in the United States
ducks for apples
at her birthday party.

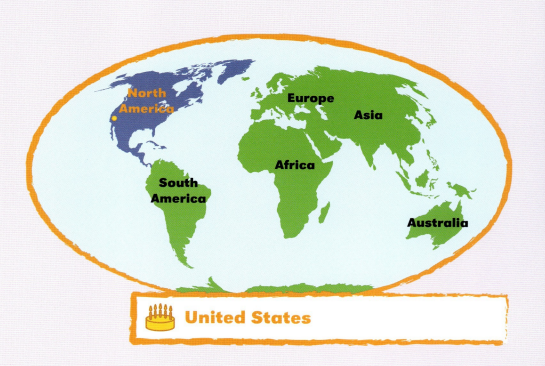

🎂 United States

A boy in Sweden
has breakfast in bed
to celebrate his birthday.

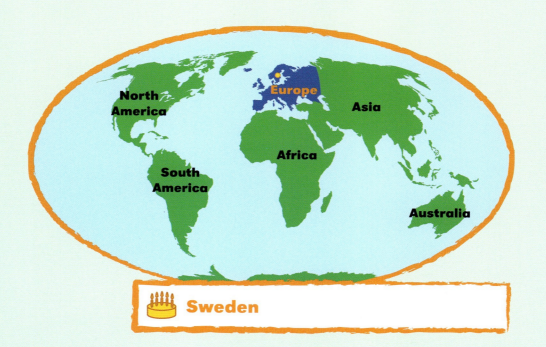

🎂 **Sweden**

# More birthday fun

A boy in South Africa
blows out candles
on his birthday cake.

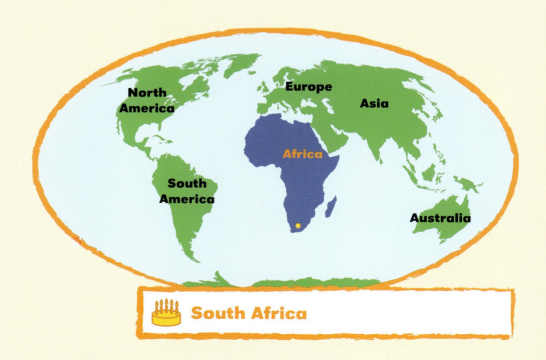

South Africa

A boy in England
goes shopping
on his birthday.

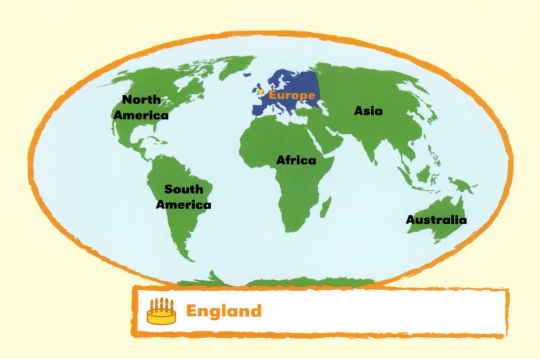

North America

Europe

Asia

Africa

South America

Australia

England

A boy in Germany
eats at a restaurant
on his birthday.

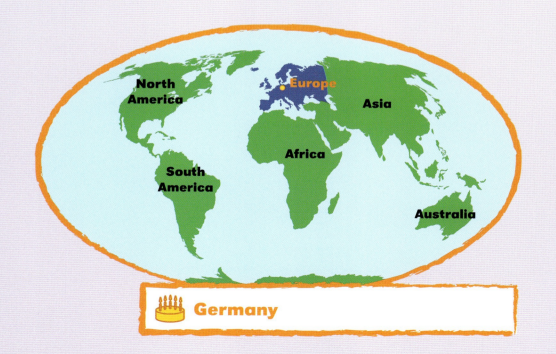

North
America

Europe

Asia

Africa

South
America

Australia

Germany

People open gifts
on their birthdays.
A girl in Mexico picks
which gift to open first.

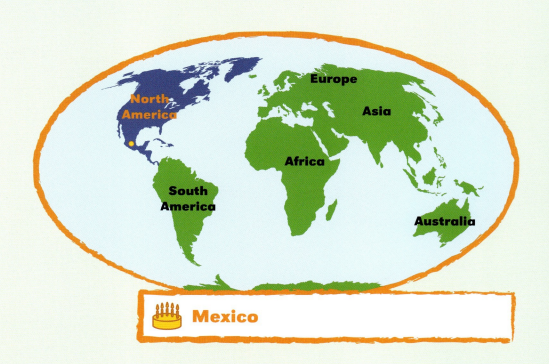

Mexico

# Your birthday

Around the world,
people laugh and play
on their birthdays.
When is your birthday?

China

# Glossary

**celebrate**  do something fun, like having a party

**culture**  way of life, ideas, customs and traditions of a group of people

**piñata**  container filled with candies and gifts; piñatas are popular at Latin American parties and celebrations

**restaurant**  place where people pay to eat meals

# Find out more

*Birthdays Around the World* (Engage in Literacy), Jay Dale (Raintree, 2012)

*Birthdays Around the World* (Bug Club), Lisa Weir (Pearson, 2016)

*Birthdays in Different Places* (Learning About Our Global Community), Lauren McNiven and Crystal Sikkens (Crabtree Publishing Co, 2016)

# Websites

www.birthdaycelebrations.net
Fun facts about birthdays around the world.

www.kidsparties.com/TraditionsInDifferentCountries.htm
Birthday traditions for people in many different countries.

# Index